Sierra de yeso

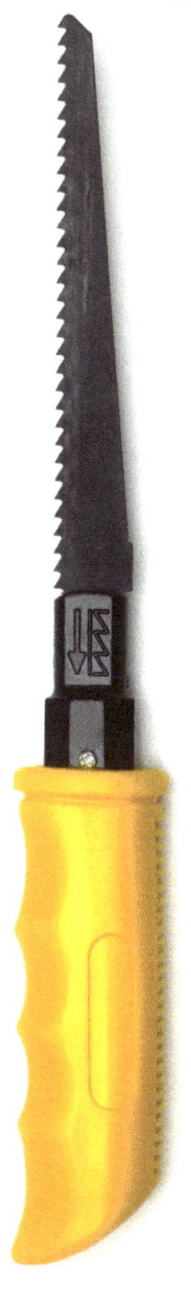

Martillo de acabado

Desarmador de cabeza plana

Martillo para marco

Guantes

Sierra para metales

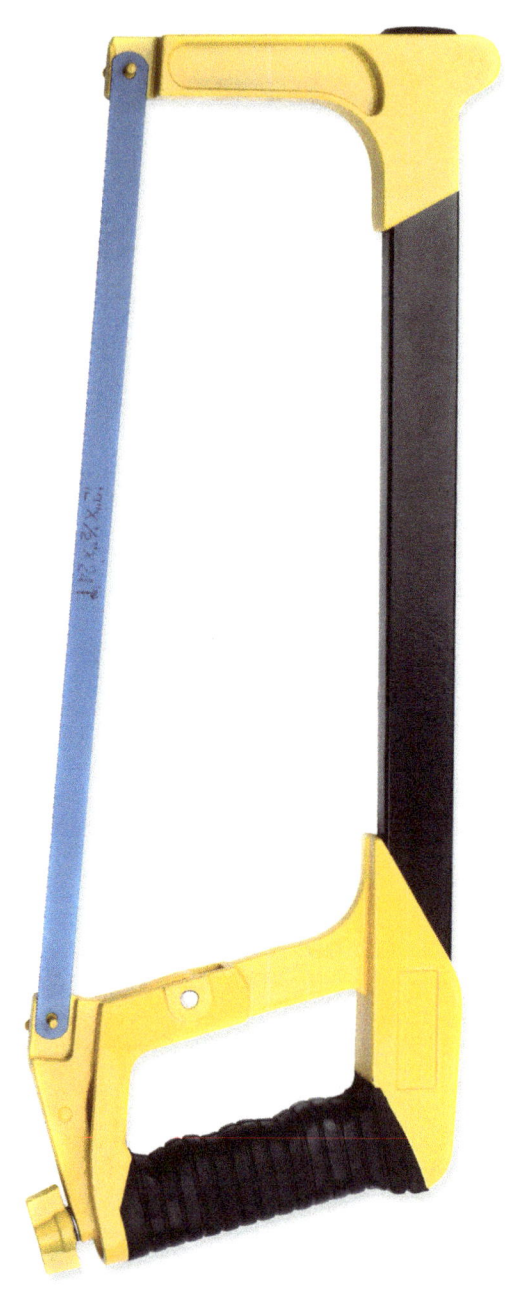

Casco

Hacha

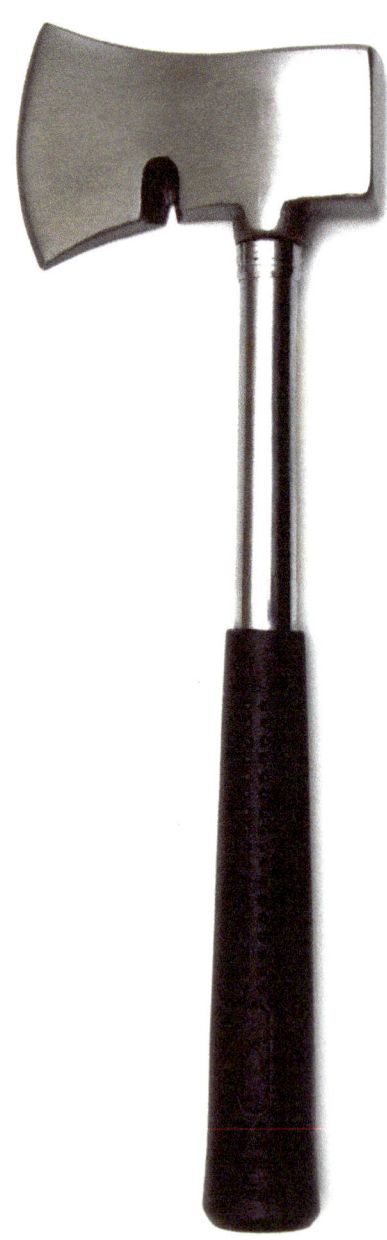

Mazo

Llave inglesa

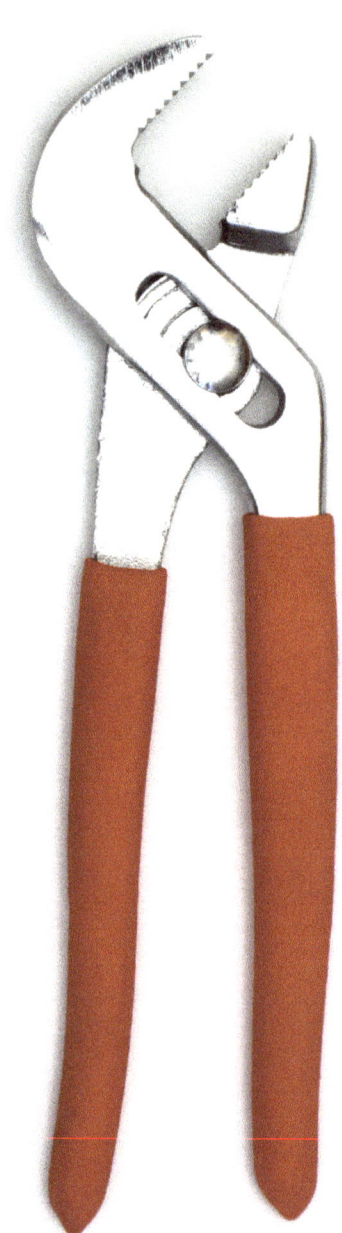

Clavos

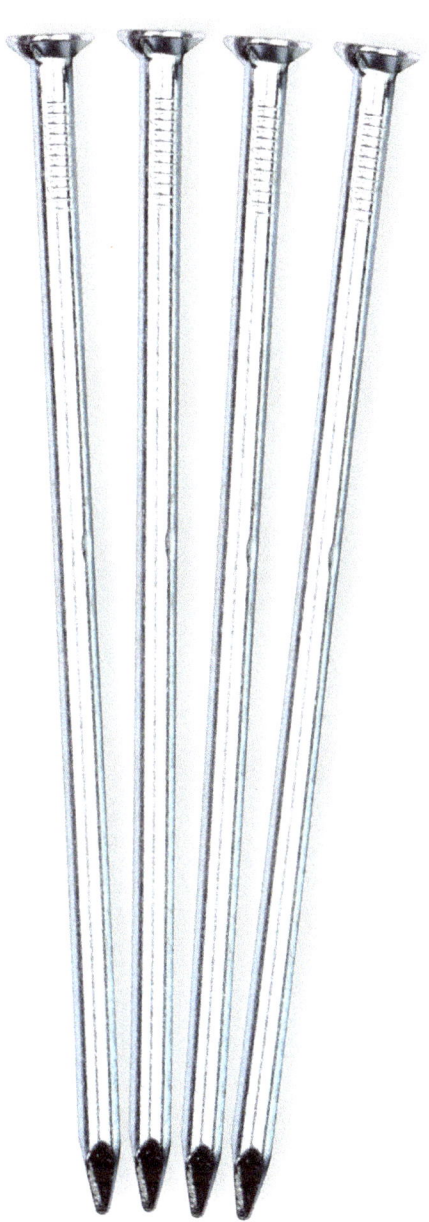

Pinzas de punta de aguja

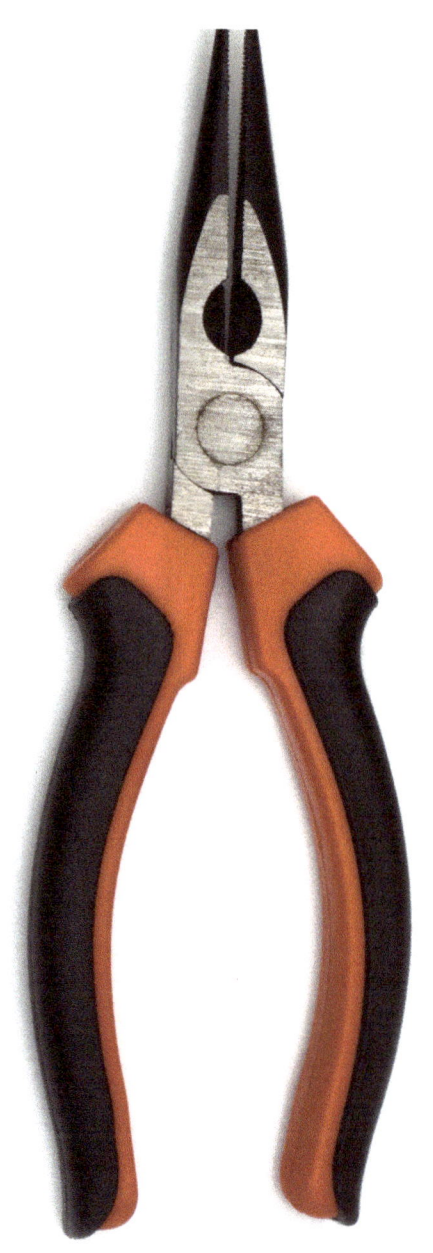

Brocha

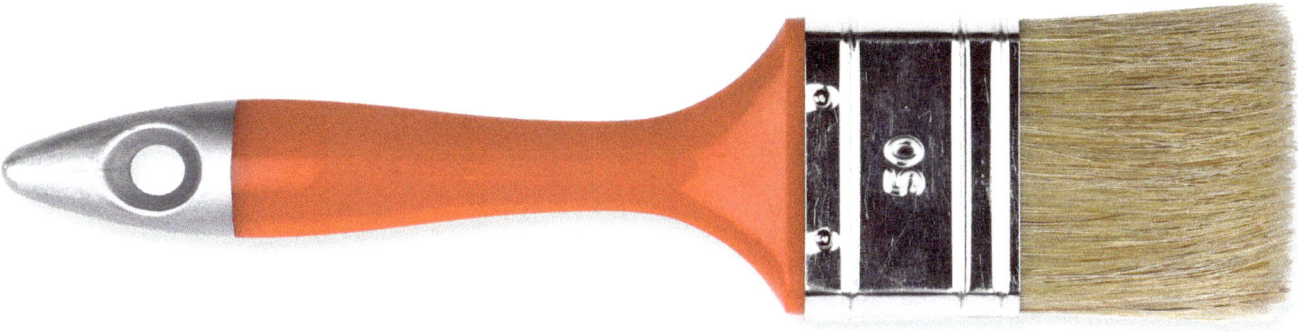

Desarmador de cruz

Pinzas

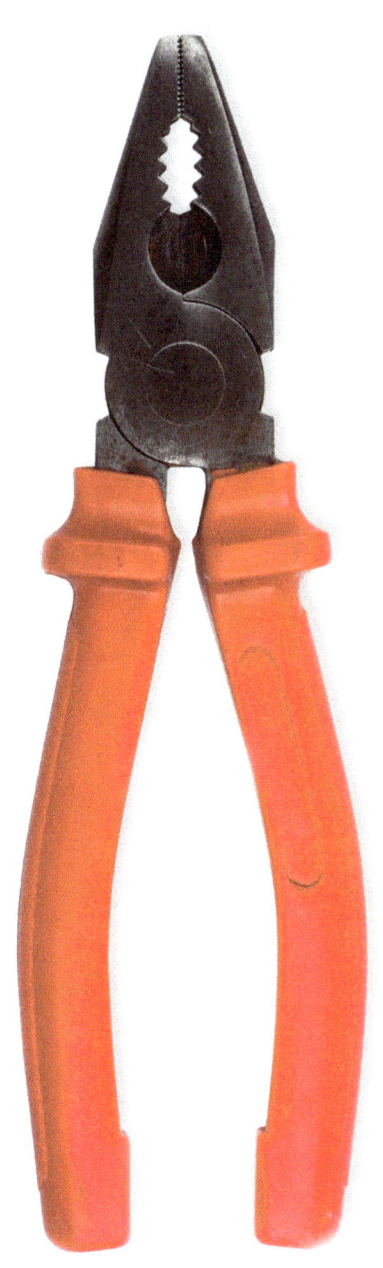

Cuchillo para macilla

Navaja

Regla

Tornillos

Pistola de grapas

Cinta Metrica

Nivelador

Desforradora de Alambres

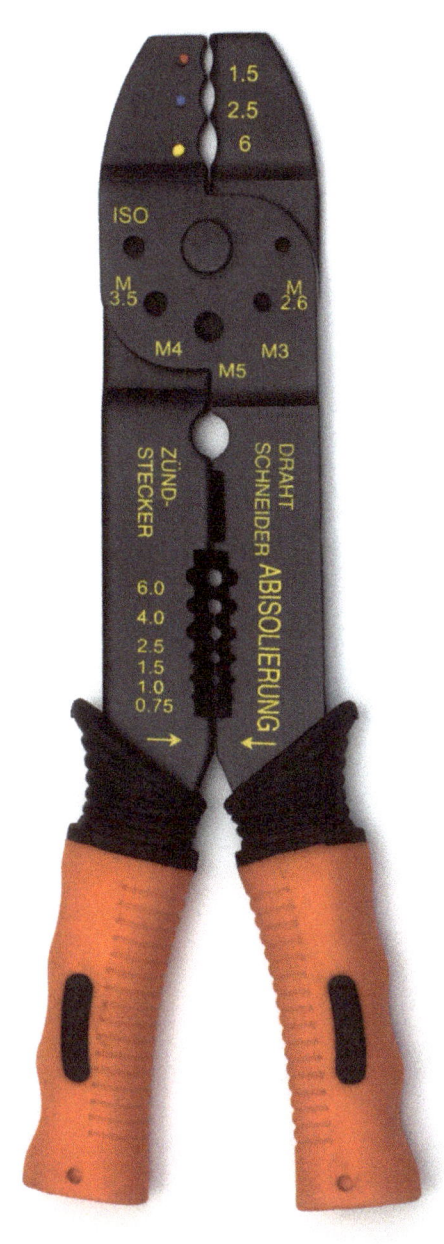

Llave inglesa

Make Sure to Check Out the Other Discover Series Books from Xist Publishing:

Published in the United States by Xist Publishing
www.xistpublishing.com
PO Box 61593 Irvine, CA 92602

© 2018 by Xist Publishing All rights reserved
Translated by Lenny Sandoval
No portion of this book may be reproduced without express permission of the publisher
All images licensed from Fotolia
First Spanish Edition

ISBN: 978-1-5324-0780-2 eISBN: 978-1-5324-0781-9